Regions of the United States: The Mid-Atlantic

Gary E. Barr

Chicago, Illinois

Produced for Raintree by
White-Thomson Publishing Ltd,
Bridgewater Business Centre,
210 High Street, Lewes, BN7 2NH

Edited by Susan Rossi Crean
Page layout by Malcolm Walker
Photo research by Stephen White-Thomson
Illustrations by John Fleck

15 14 13 12 11
10 9 8 7 6 5 4 3 2 1

Library of Congress Cataloging-in-Publication Data

Barr, Gary, 1951-
  The Mid-Atlantic / Gary E. Barr.
    p. cm. -- (Regions of the USA)
  Includes bibliographical references and index.
  ISBN 1-4109-2307-X (hc) -- ISBN 1-4109-2315-0 (pb)
  1. Middle Atlantic States--Juvenile literature. I. Title. II. Series.

F106.B37 2007
974--dc22
                            2006004694

Acknowledgements
The publisher would like to thank the following for permission to reproduce photographs:
pp. 4, 8, 9, 15, 26, 30, 31, 33, 37, 41, 43, 45, 50, 51 Jeffrey Greenberg; p. 5 Annie Griffiths/Corbis Belt; pp. 6, 17, 27B Gibson Stock Photography; p. 10 National Park Service/Gettysburg National Military Park; p. 11 Historical Picture Archive/Corbis; p. 12 Stinkyt/I-stock; p. 13 David Grossman/The Image Works/Topfoto; pp. 16, 18, 20, 22, 23, 27A, 35, 36, 40, 42, 48, 49 Viesti Associates; p. 19 Reuters/Corbis; p. 21 Vladimir Ivanov/I-stock; Pietro Valdinoci/I-stock; p. 25A Corbis; Dave Huss/I-stock; p. 28 Topfoto; pp. 29, 39 David Frazier; p. 34 David Zimmerman/Corbis; p. 38 Gary Gladstone/Corbis; p. 44A Mitchell Layton/NewSport/Corbis; p. 44B Icon SMI/Corbis; p. 46 David Brooks/Corbis p.47 James Leynse/Corbis.

Every effort has been made to contact copyright holders of any material reproduced in this book. Any omissions will be rectified in subsequent printings if notice is given to the publisher.

Cover photo of Manhattan skyline, New York reproduced with permission of I-stock

Contents

Some words are shown in bold, **like this**. You can find out what they mean by looking in the glossary.

The Mid-Atlantic

Skyscrapers

Nowhere in the United States can you see as many skyscrapers as in New York City. Chicago is usually identified as the city with the first skyscraper. It has a little more than 1,500 such structures compared to more than 5,900 found in New York City. By building upward, more people can live and work in heavily populated cities.

Along the northeast coast of this region you can find a **cluster** of cities so heavily populated that they are all connected. Right at the **borders** of one city the next city begins. This chain of cities includes New York City; Philadelphia, Pennsylvania; Baltimore, Maryland; and Washington DC.

This chain of cities is found in the Mid-Atlantic. The region is so-named because the states in it are located midway along the east coast of the United States, along the Atlantic Ocean. This region has almost one-fifth of the total population of the United States, numerous **ethnic groups**, and the U.S. capital, Washington DC.

Students gaze at skyscrapers located in Manhattan, a **borough** of New York City.

Diverse people, diverse land

In other parts of the Mid-Atlantic, beaches, bays, waterfalls, and other landforms can be found. For example, just as a ridge of big cities with large skyscrapers forms the northeast border of the Mid-Atlantic, a ridge of mountains lines the southwest of the region. The Blue Ridge Mountains of Virginia have rugged slopes with beautiful trees, abundant wildlife, and few people.

While much of the Mid-Atlantic is industrial and **urban**, the southwest sections belong to the rural, southern culture of the United States. Numerous job opportunities and recreational sites are found in this area.

The Chesapeake Bay, one of the region's most important water features, is located in Maryland.
▼

Find out later...

What does this painting portray?

What takes place inside the U.S. Capitol?

Which famous university is this?

Chain of cities

The seven states of the Mid-Atlantic region cover less than 5 percent of the area of the United States but contain almost 20 percent of the nation's population. Some parts of the Mid-Atlantic are very crowded.

If you view Earth from space, part of this region would show up very brightly. That's because a huge **megalopolis** is located along the coast of the Mid-Atlantic states. It is an area where a 300-mile (482-kilometer) chain of cities has formed. This occurred when several cities expanded until they grew together. With so many people and city structures present, lights from the area have a bright appearance at night.

These students are hearing about Ellis Island near Manhattan, where many immigrants first entered the United States.

CANADA

NEW YORK

•Buffalo

☆Albany

PENNSYLVANIA

Newark•   •New York City

Pittsburgh•

Harrisburg☆

☆Trenton

Philadelphia•

NEW JERSEY

MARYLAND

WEST VIRGINIA

Annapolis•

☆Dover

DELAWARE

☆Charleston

DISTRICT OF COLUMBIA

VIRGINIA

Richmond☆

Norfolk•

N
W   E
S

0   200 miles
0   300 kilometers

Immigrants arrive

In the 1600s, Europeans moved to the Mid-Atlantic in great numbers. Great harbors and large rivers allowed these settlers to trade goods easily. The region's harbors welcomed millions of **immigrants** in the late 1800s and early 1900s. Today, as in the past, businesses continue to locate here because they can ship goods efficiently to customers. As a result, jobs have been plentiful in the Mid-Atlantic.

Fact file

State	Population	Size
Delaware	783,600	2,045 sq. mi. (5,297 sq. km)
Maryland	5,296,486	10,460 sq. mi. (27,091 sq. km)
New Jersey	8,414,350	7,787 sq. mi. (20,168 sq. km)
New York	18,976,457	49,108 sq. mi. (127,189 sq. km)
Pennsylvania	12,281,054	44,819 sq. mi. (116,080 sq. km)
Virginia	7,078,515	36,597 sq. mi. (94,786 sq. km)
West Virginia	1,808,344	24,086 sq. mi. (62,382 sq. km)

People and History

The Mohawks

Mohawks live mostly in northern New York and bordering areas of Canada. They were once part of the Iroquois (Haudenosaunee) Nation. Mohawks tried to stay out of the Revolutionary War (1775–1783), but eventually sided with the British because they feared American settlers would take their lands. After the conflict, they were forced to leave most of their lands and move north to Canada.

Native Americans were the Mid-Atlantic's first residents. They lived in the region for thousands of years before the first settlers arrived from England in 1607. The Powhatans greeted these first settlers. At first, Native Americans of the Mid-Atlantic welcomed the English, trading and teaching them survival skills. However, disagreements over land and lifestyles eventually caused conflicts.

By the 1800s, few Native Americans remained. Huge numbers died from European diseases, while others died during violent clashes such as the **French and Indian War**. Names of places such as Mohawk Valley and Shenandoah River are some of the few reminders of the Native-American cultures that once flourished in the Mid-Atlantic.

A copy of an early Native American home along the Blue Ridge Parkway in Virginia contains woven materials and a smoke hole. ▼

Heart of the colonies

The first permanent English settlement was established at Jamestown. It grew to be the colony of Virginia. Virginia would play an important role in the American Revolution that ended British rule and formed the United States. Important battles of the American Revolution were fought in New York, Pennsylvania, New Jersey, and Virginia.

Philadelphia

Philadelphia was where the United States was founded. The Declaration of Independence was adopted in Philadelphia's Independence Hall in 1776 and the United States Constitution was written there in 1787. Philadelphia was the nation's capital from 1790 until 1800. Today, Philadelphia remains an important cultural and business center for the United States.

A reconstructed log cabin in Tidewater, Virginia, shows what life in the colonies may have been like. ▼

Fact file
Eight U.S. presidents were born in Virginia.

The Civil War

Many Civil War (1861–1865) battles were fought in Mid-Atlantic states. Almost half of the 636,000 soldiers who died in the war fell in Virginia, a **Confederate** state. The largest battle of the war was at Gettysburg, Pennsylvania, in 1863. Here, **Union** forces stopped Confederate soldiers after a three-day battle that caused over 50,000 casualties. West Virginia became a state in 1863 during the Civil War, after it broke away from the Confederate state Virginia.

A growing nation

A huge wave of immigrants arrived in the years just before and after 1900 at Ellis Island in New York City. This is where examinations were done to either allow people to enter the United States or be forced to return to their native land. Of those accepted, many settled in the Mid-Atlantic region. They took part in the **Industrial Revolution** of the late 1800s, when large factories were built.

This painting depicts the surrender of the Confederacy to the Union during the Civil War.

Fact file

West Virginia is the only state in the country to break off from another state.

10

Industrial revolution

During the Industrial Revolution, **seaports** and cities on rivers that were located near **natural resources** grew into great factory cities. Pittsburgh and Philadelphia in Pennsylvania, New York City, and Baltimore, Maryland produced huge amounts of steel, machinery, and other finished goods. Today, descendants of immigrant groups still work and live in the Mid-Atlantic and keep their ethnic groups' history alive.

Changing businesses

By the 1970s, factory production in the Mid-Atlantic began to decrease. Foreign companies produced factory goods for lower prices than ones made in the Mid-Atlantic. Steel mills and other factories began to shut down in the region, while businesses involved with insurance, banking, and computers grew.

Early American cities such as New York were mostly located on coasts or near rivers for trade.

⌄

September 11

Terrorists attacked Mid-Atlantic sites on September 11, 2001. Two jetliners crashed into and destroyed New York City's World Trade Towers—two of the world's tallest buildings. Another jet smashed into the Pentagon building in Washington DC. A fourth plane went down in rural Pennsylvania when passengers stopped terrorists from reaching their target. Altogether, over 3,000 Americans lost their lives in these attacks.

Polish Pittsburgh

Ethnic neighborhoods are popular in Mid-Atlantic cities. One in Pittsburgh called Polish Hill dates to 1896 and is an example of how immigrants formed neighborhoods. Polish residents helped newcomers adjust to life in America while keeping their traditions alive. Polish Hill has seen both good and tough times, but it remains an important site for Polish people in Pittsburgh.

Everyday life

Throughout the Mid-Atlantic there are many **descendants** of immigrants who came to the United States from the 1600s through the 1900s. This includes large numbers of people with German, Irish, Italian, African-American, and English ancestry. For example, in Pennsylvania, 25.4 percent of people living there are of German descent, 16 percent are of Irish descent, and 10 percent are African American. Less than 1 percent of the people living in the Mid-Atlantic region are Native American.

In the Mid-Atlantic, people who have moved into this region work and go to school with people from all around the world.

The Statue of Liberty in New York's harbor is an important symbol of freedom for Americans.

New immigrants

The Mid-Atlantic is as much a region of new immigrants as it is a region of descendants of settlers and earlier immigrants. For example, about 20 percent of the population of the state of New York was born in other countries.

Many new immigrants move to Fairfax, Virginia. This city is close to Washington DC. As the national government and high technology businesses of the area expand, many new immigrants find jobs there. Unlike many areas of the United States where most immigrants come from just a few nations, Fairfax has immigrants from many different nations.

International school

At one Mid-Atlantic high school in Falls Church, Virginia, students speak more than 30 different languages. In recent years, half of JEB Stuart High School's 1,400 students were foreign born. For the most part, the attitude among students is one of hope for the future. Many students express appreciation for the place they now live while gaining an education at the school. Many of the new immigrants here have dreams and wants that are similar to those of immigrants who arrived in the Mid-Atlantic 400 years ago.

A piper plays ◀ the bagpipes at New York's St. Patrick's Day Parade, one of many international events held there each year.

Land in the Area

Coastal waters

More important estuaries are found in the Mid-Atlantic region than in any other part of the United States. The calm waters in the estuaries provide great locations for harbors such as those found in Philadelphia, Pennsylvania, and Norfolk, Virginia. Estuaries' currents can be so slow that seawater flows into rivers. Water levels rise and fall like ocean tides, as in eastern Virginia where the land is called "The Tidewater."

Even with its huge cities, there is plenty of land in the Mid-Atlantic. The land is both varied and beautiful. Within a few hours, people can drive from the large cities across flat plains, over rolling hills, and arrive at remote, colorful mountains. The Appalachian Mountains cross five Mid-Atlantic states and vary in size from about 2,000 to 6,000 feet (610 to 1,829 meters) above sea level. Several large rivers empty into the Atlantic Ocean in the Mid-Atlantic region. Along the coast there are beaches, numerous bays, and **estuaries**.

Fact file
Maryland has 3,200 miles (5,150 kilometers) of shoreline.

Lake Huron

Lake Ontario

NEW YORK

Erie Canal

Hudson R.

Lake Erie

PENNSYLVANIA

Susquehanna R.

Delaware R.

NEW JERSEY

MARYLAND DELAWARE

Delaware Bay

Potomac R.

WEST VIRGINIA

VIRGINIA

James R.

Chesapeake Bay

ATLANTIC OCEAN

N
W   E
S

- 1,800–3,000 ft. (549–1,829 m)
- 1,200–1,800 ft. (366–549 m)
- 600–1,200 ft. (183–366 m)
- 150–600 ft. (56–183 m)
- 0–150 ft. (0–56 m)

0   200 miles
0   300 kilometers

Plains and hills

Bordering the Atlantic Ocean are the coastal plains. Narrow in New York, they gradually widen to the south. Delaware is an example of how flat these lands are. It has a maximum elevation of 448 feet (137 meters) above sea level.

West of the coastal plains lies the piedmont **plateau,** found in Virginia, Maryland, and Pennsylvania. It is hilly land between 200 and 600 feet (61 and 183 meters) above sea level. The fall line is a place where rivers form waterfalls and rapids as they quickly drop from the piedmont onto the coastal plains.

Mile markers can be found along the Appalachian Trail in places such as Shenandoah National Park in Virginia.

▶

Age of the Appalachians

Estimated to be 600 million years old, the Appalachian Mountains are considered to be some of the oldest mountains on Earth. They are believed to have formed when giant pieces of the earth's crust collided. Once 15,000 feet (4,572 meters) above sea level, water and wind erosion has worn most down to about one-third their original height.

Niagara Falls

Niagara Falls is famous for its beauty and power, not just its 160-foot (29-meter) height. It has the sixth largest amount of water of any waterfall in the world. Tourists can experience the beauty and power of the falls from several viewpoints. When the water hits rocks at the bottom of the falls, it sprays high into the air, sometimes drenching tourists.

Seaports

New York City's harbor, at the **mouths** of the Hudson and East Rivers, is among the busiest in the world. Because ships are able to carry huge amounts of goods, many large companies are located in New York so they can sell worldwide. Baltimore, Maryland and Philadelphia, Pennsylvania, are two other seaport cities of the region. Philadelphia is located where the Delaware and Schuylkill Rivers meet. Baltimore is located near the northern coast of the Chesapeake Bay. Like New York, both of these cities grew to be prosperous business centers.

Niagara Falls in New York is a major tourist site. ▼

Naval and river ports

Norfolk, Virginia, contains the world's largest naval base. Near two estuaries at the southern end of the Chesapeake Bay, and midway along the Atlantic Coast, it is an ideal position. Naval ships are built in the area and dock there. Buffalo, New York, on Lake Erie and Pittsburgh, Pennsylvania, on the Ohio River, have ports that transport goods to cities deep in the interior of the United States.

Tourists can board some of the naval vessels such as the USS *Wisconsin* in Norfolk, Virginia.

▼

Baltimore Aquarium

The Baltimore Aquarium contains more than 10,500 creatures. It includes stingrays, sharks, dolphins, and sea turtles. Students from all around the eastern United States go to the aquarium on field trips. In addition to the many aquatic exhibits, they enjoy seeing special shows such as those with leaping dolphins.

Flash floods are a major problem in West Virginia. Most of the state is very hilly. Hundreds of streams and rivers flow through narrow, steep-sided valleys. When heavy rains occur, these rivers rise quickly and can cause great amounts of destruction. Fast-flowing streams can become deadly.

Climate

Parts of New York and Pennsylvania experience cold and snowy winters. Snowy weather can also be found in mountainous areas of the region. There are many ski resorts in the Appalachian Mountains. These mountain ski areas are found all the way to the southern border of Virginia. At lower elevations, the rest of the region is average in both temperature and **precipitation** levels.

Average temperatures in the Mid-Atlantic vary from the low 30s °F (around 0 °C) in January to the low 80s °F (around 27 °C) in July. Normally, the further a place is from the Atlantic Ocean, the greater the difference is between summer and winter temperatures. In the southeastern portion of the Mid-Atlantic, yearly average temperatures are slightly higher.

▲
Hilly land, steep mountain slopes, and occasional heavy rain can cause flash floods in places such as West Virginia.

Precipitation

Most precipitation occurs during the summer in the Mid-Atlantic states. Average rainfall ranges from 35–45 inches (90–114 centimeters) per year. This is plenty of moisture for the area's plant life to flourish. A blue haze appears above Virginia's forested mountains because of moisture rising from thick forests. The Blue Ridge Mountains were named for this blue haze.

Blizzards, especially at locations near the Great Lakes, can lead to large snowfalls. Areas within 100 miles (161 kilometers) of Lake Erie and Lake Ontario's eastern shores frequently experience blizzards during the winter months of January and February.

Buffalo, New York, is located in a region sometimes called the "snow belt," where lake-effect snows are common.

Lake-effect snow

The process that causes **lake-effect snow** starts when large bodies of water are warmer than cold air above them. Clouds filled with frozen moisture can easily form in this situation. Winds then blow the moisture-filled clouds onto land areas and in winter heavy snows occur. Lake Erie and Lake Ontario both cause lake-effect snow in New York and northern Pennsylvania.

Animals and Plants

Chesapeake Crab

There are more than 295 species of fish known to occur in the Chesapeake Bay region. The blue crab is the most famous and many people say the most delicious. Aquatic life, such as the Chesapeake blue crab, has been important to the area's food supply for many years. Native Americans showed European settlers how to catch and eat crab.

The highly populated areas of the Mid-Atlantic have forced wildlife into smaller **habitat** areas. Some isolated areas of New York have moose, but most of the animals in Mid-Atlantic states are small. Squirrels, rabbits, deer, and other small mammals are found in every section of the Mid-Atlantic. Many types of birds such as robins, crows, cardinals, and hawks live in the region.

Wetland marshes around the Chesapeake Bay cover 250,000 acres. They purify water entering the bay, help prevent floods, and provide homes for 3,600 species of plants and animals. Pollution from the 16 million people living around the bay threatens these areas.

Many Mid-Atlantic residents enjoy catching and eating blue crabs, but here they are being entertained with a "crab race."

Invaders

Invasive species have made their way into several areas of the Mid-Atlantic. Animals from faraway places are often brought accidentally on ships or aircraft. When they invade habitats, they can be extremely destructive. Invasive insects such as woodwasps and plants such as kudzu kill trees. Parts of southern Virginia have been affected very much by kudzu.

The invasive snakehead fish, which was first brought into the United States as an aquarium fish, eats large quantities of native fish. Snakehead fish have been found in this region in the Potomac River.

Deer and other wildlife are a common site in Shenandoah National Park in Virginia.

Dismal Swamp

Located in southeastern Virginia, Dismal Swamp is a place with a large number of birds and aquatic life. In the past, when horses were used for transportation, the area got its name because it was difficult to travel through. Covering over 100,000 acres of land, it is one of the largest wilderness areas near the Atlantic Coast in the United States.

Rich plant life

Tourists travel long distances to see the beautiful forests, wildflowers, and wetlands located in the Mid-Atlantic region. Thick forests of trees such as oak and maple thrive throughout the region. In spring, their light green leaves form a **canopy** for the blooming white dogwood trees that grow underneath. Before losing their leaves in the fall, these trees turn beautiful shades of red, yellow, and orange. Pine trees are found on mountains and in northern sections of the Mid-Atlantic.

The fall colors make this image of a mill in West Virginia look more like a painting than a photo.
▼

Other plants

Under trees and in grassy areas, wild plants thrive. Ferns and mosses grow well in dark recesses of the forests. Wildflowers and bushes grow well in sunny areas. Pink mountain laurel adds color to Appalachian slopes in early summer.

New Jersey's Pine Barrens region is a strange mixture of small pines, swamps, and salt marshes. Covering over one million acres, the "Barrens" contain wild cranberries, blueberries, and birds. It is the largest coastal wilderness of the Mid-Atlantic region. Equally important, under the Pine Barrens is the biggest fresh-water reservoir on the East Coast.

The New River mostly flows through wilderness areas. Here it cuts through a gorge as it flows north through West Virginia. ▲

What happened to chestnut trees?

The American chestnut used to be one of the great trees of Mid-Atlantic forests. These trees grew to be 100 feet (30.48 meters) high and were used to make furniture, to supply sap for **tanning** leather, and to provide nuts for food. A disease killed American chestnut trees between 1904 and 1945. Today, young chestnut trees may occasionally sprout but they do not grow very large and are usually killed by the same disease. It is believed that plants brought from a foreign nation infected the chestnuts.

Cities and Towns

Adding a dome

The first Capitol Building finished in 1811 had no dome. This feature was added in 1819, but it was not very impressive. In 1863 the current dome was finished. This dome is one of the largest on Earth and makes the structure one of the most recognizable buildings in the United States.

The large cities of the Mid-Atlantic are alike in some ways, but they are also very different. Some of the cities grew out of the Industrial Revolution, while others have grown more recently. Some grew as capital cities, including the nation's capital—Washington DC.

In 1790 Congress chose a location on the Potomac River between Maryland and Virginia for the national capital. The federal government moved to Washington in 1800, but it took many years to become the city that Pierre L'Enfant, its original designer, had in mind. L'Enfant placed the Capitol Building in Washington's center. This is where members of Congress pass national laws.

The Capitol Building's huge dome and location on a hill in Washington DC give it a great presence.

Government and cultural center

There are many important government offices in Washington DC. The Pentagon is the headquarters for the military, the State Department is the center for **foreign policy**, and the Justice Department deals with policing citizens. Pennsylvania Avenue connects the Capitol with the White House, which is where the president lives. Also nearby is the Supreme Court, the highest court in the land.

Besides government locations, Washington DC is a place to see cultural sites. The National Gallery of Art, the Kennedy Center, and Georgetown University are examples of art, music, and academic sites found in the nation's capital.

The Pentagon is a five-sided building that houses the nation's Department of Defense. ▶

Working as a page

Pages are high school or college students chosen for their academic and citizenship achievements. They work with senators and members of the House of Representatives to run errands and do other tasks. In return, pages get to meet famous people and learn about how government works.

The White ◀ House lawn covers several acres. The president's Oval Office is in the center on the second floor.

New York City

With 8 million people, New York City has the highest population of any city in the country. It is also the nation's most important business center. New York's busy financial district includes the **New York Stock Exchange**. It is also a main seaport, the headquarters of the **United Nations**, and a center for the fashion, publishing, entertainment, and advertising industries.

New York City is known as an artistic and cultural center. From musicals, plays, and performances on Broadway to museums such as the Metropolitan Museum of Art and the Children's Museum of Manhattan, New York City's cultural offerings are many and varied.

Famous streets of New York City

Wall Street is in the heart of New York City's banking and financial district. Fifth Avenue is a well-known shopping district. Broadway has many famous theaters, and Park Avenue has several advertising companies.

New York's Central Park provides relief from the noisy city surrounding it. Central Park includes many features including Bethesda Fountain shown here.

Philadelphia

Philadelphia has always held a special place in U.S. culture. It was the site where the two most important documents in the United States were written—The Declaration of Independence and the Constitution of the United States.

The University of Pennsylvania is one of several respected universities in Philadelphia. The Academy of Natural Sciences is a research center and museum with ancient fossils and living exotic animals. Located near where the Delaware and Schuylkill Rivers meet, Philadelphia is also a busy business and port city.

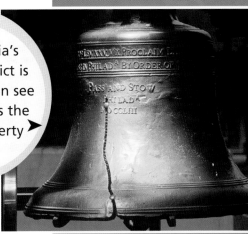

Philadelphia's historic district is where you can see items such as the original Liberty Bell.

A statue of Philadelphia's most famous resident, Ben Franklin, graces a busy highway. Franklin was witty, inventive, and patriotic.

Historic landmarks

A lot of tourists visit Philadelphia's many historic sites each year. Among the most popular attractions are Independence Hall, the Liberty Bell, and the Betsy Ross House. Independence Hall contains meeting rooms where the Declaration of Independence was adopted and the Constitution was written. The Betsy Ross House has materials belonging to the woman who designed the U.S. flag. The buildings are so near to each other in some parts of the city that walking between them makes people feel like they are living in the 1700s.

Purpose-built parks

Many Mid-Atlantic cities are now attempting to use a checkerboard pattern of **green spaces**, business districts, and residential areas. Parks and natural areas add beauty, recreation areas, and a less-crowded feeling to cities. Alexandria, Virginia, for example, provides plenty of open spaces, with 127 parks for its residents.

Small towns

Small Mid-Atlantic towns often have long, rich histories. For example, in 1683, the site for Princeton, New Jersey, was a stopover along a road to New York City. A college moved to the small farm community in 1756.

Today, many of Princeton's 14,000 people travel a one-hour journey to New York City to work. Princeton is more than just a stopover place now. It has an attractive downtown area, parks, elegant housing, and one of the world's greatest universities—Princeton University.

Princeton University students enjoy the sun. Woodrow Wilson taught here and James Madison graduated from Princeton before they became presidents.

Fact file

New Jersey is the country's most crowded state, with over 1,000 people per square mile (2.6 square kilometer).

A changing community

Abingdon, Virginia, dates back to the mid-1700s. A small logging community, it was burned by Union troops during the Civil War. In 1933 a young Virginian moved to Abingdon and started the Barter Theater, where farmers could trade goods to see plays. Along with the Barter Theater, Abingdon also attracts tourists to the Blue Ridge Mountains. The town of 7,800 has switched from timbering and farming to tourism, producing craft items, and providing services.

Living close to work

The main reasons people reside in a place are jobs, housing preferences, environment for children, transportation, and climate. Jobs are the most important attraction. A person's job is central to their survival in today's world. Throughout its history, the Mid-Atlantic has been able to offer numerous job opportunities. The result is a high population.

Williamsburg, Virginia, is one of the most famous small towns of the Mid-Atlantic. It welcomes millions of history-seeking tourists each year.

Rural Life

Mad about mushrooms

Pennsylvania leads the nation in mushroom production. Almost half of the mushrooms produced in the United States come from this state. The mushrooms grow in dark, underground specially-designed "mushroom houses."

The Mid-Atlantic states use less land for farming than any other U.S. region. Sprawling cities and **suburbs** limit the amount of land available for growing crops. Even so, some Mid-Atlantic states are known for their production of certain agricultural products. For example, New York ranks third and Pennsylvania ranks fourth in dairy production. New York, Virginia, and Pennsylvania also rank high among states in production of apples, cabbage, mushrooms, corn, and tomatoes.

The Mid-Atlantic is "garden country." Most people keep gardens for fun, but some also profit from their work.

Practical produce

A truck farm is a farm that is close enough to a city for freshly picked **produce** to be brought in by trucks. Truck farms located in New Jersey supply New York City along the state's northern border and Philadelphia along its southern border. Some truck farms sell to grocery stores, some to restaurants, and others sell directly by setting up stands along roadways.

Amish life

In 1681 William Penn founded Pennsylvania as a place where Quakers could follow their religious beliefs. The Quakers believe in living simple lives, but **Amish** beliefs are stricter. The Amish believe in living without modern conveniences. They have no electricity in their homes and do not own motorized vehicles.

Going west

Some of the first major movements west of the Appalachian Mountains occurred because of the need for farmland. When good farmland had all been purchased by the mid-1700s in Pennsylvania, landless settlers began moving southwest into Virginia's valleys. Again, land became scarce and farmers followed a route that crossed into Kentucky and other areas west of the mountains to find new farmland.

Amish farmers use traditional methods of farming. Pennsylvania and other Mid-Atlantic states are home to many Amish. ▼

Getting Around

Going by water

Freight can be carried by water from Mid-Atlantic states far into the interior of the country. For example, from New York City's harbor, goods can go north by boat on the Hudson River to the Erie Canal. There they can turn west and make it to the Great Lakes, and eventually be transported to the Mississippi River, all the way to New Orleans.

There are ▶ more interstate highways per square mile in this area than in any other U.S. region.

The Mid-Atlantic states have numerous highways, extensive rail systems, busy airports, and large seaport and river-port facilities. The area's products have to be efficiently transported to customers, or business will suffer. The region's factories and workers depend on the **raw materials** transported into the area.

Trucks are quick ways to send goods from Mid-Atlantic ports and factories to consumers. Conversely, trucks bring goods for overseas shipping, raw materials for factories, and finished products for stores to Mid-Atlantic locations.

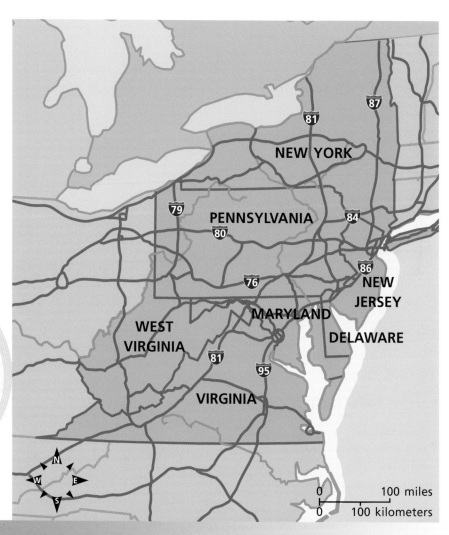

Heavy congestion

In the megalopolis, traffic is very congested. Of the longest **commutes** to work in the nation, three occur in Mid-Atlantic cities. The average commute in New York City is 38.3 minutes; in Newark, New Jersey, it is 31.5 minutes; and in Philadelphia it is 29.4 minutes. Use of subway systems, carpooling, and other methods of transportation are being promoted to ease traffic.

In some large cities of the Mid-Atlantic, many people choose not to own a car. They can get around their city by using public transportation such as subways and buses. Many people can walk to shopping areas, jobs, and entertainment areas. People can also travel to their destination by paying a driver to take them there in a taxi.

Many people in New York don't own cars. Instead, people there depend on taxis and other forms of transportation.

Amazing planes

Dover Air Force Base in Delaware houses the world's largest military planes. C-5 Galaxies were designed to transport large amounts of military equipment quickly. For example, the C-5 can carry 270,000 pounds (12,247 kilograms) of equipment. To lift such loads, the combined energy of its four engines is strong enough to power 3,000 automobiles.

Work in the Area

Electric company

In 1876 Thomas Edison established a new laboratory in Menlo Park, New Jersey. His inventions helped to grow electric use in the United States. Today, work involved with electricity is one of the biggest industries of the Mid-Atlantic. Hundreds of thousands of electrical technicians are employed in New Jersey and other states of the region.

Important seaports employ many people living in the Mid-Atlantic. Baltimore, Maryland, is one of the most important **seaports** in the United States. Located on the Chesapeake Bay, it is well protected from storms and high waves. Docks are often located in bays so waves do not disrupt the safe transfer of cargo.

Baltimore's harbor on the Chesapeake Bay provides docks for naval vessels, cruise liners, fishing boats, and pleasure boats.
▼

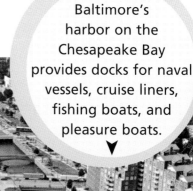

Working in the water

People have fished in the Chesapeake Bay for hundreds of years. The Chesapeake Bay is actually a 200-mile- (322-kilometer-) long estuary. The bay connects Mid-Atlantic rivers with the Atlantic Ocean. The primary fish caught there are striped bass, perch, and catfish. The most valuable shellfish are blue crabs, but they also harvest oysters and clams.

"Watermen," the Chesapeake area term for independent fishers, is a proud title. Watermen harvest blue crabs during summer, oysters in fall, and a variety of fish in the winter months.

Boats used for catching crabs and other shellfish can easily enter shallow areas of the Chesapeake Bay.

▼

Saving the bay

Overfishing and pollution in the Chesapeake Bay are threatening the future of the area. Several groups are trying to lower pollution, improve fishing methods, and protect the natural environment of the Chesapeake Bay. They include groups such as Save the Bay and state and national government agencies.

Using resources

One of the most important natural resources in the Mid-Atlantic is coal. Huge supplies of coal exist in West Virginia, Pennsylvania, and parts of Virginia. Formed by ancient decayed plants, coal has been an important resource in this region for more than 100 years. Coal has been used for many years as a fuel to melt iron and other materials in the steel-making process. It is one of the reasons why so many steel mills were built in areas near Pittsburgh and Philadelphia, Pennsylvania; Baltimore, Maryland; and other locations in the Mid-Atlantic.

Trains that carry coal from mining areas each day are important to Mid-Atlantic steel mills. ▼

Fact file
The first oil well in the United States was located in Pennsylvania.

Renewable resources

Mid-Atlantic states have begun finding new energy sources. Fossil fuels such as coal and oil are non-renewable. This means they cannot be replaced after they are used. Dams have been built along fast-flowing rivers in the mountains of Virginia, West Virginia, and other sites to generate power from rushing water.

Solar panels use heat from the sun to help heat some homes in the region. In some places windmills generate power. Solar, water, and wind power are **renewable**. Many jobs were created in the region to build and maintain these facilities.

Hard work, close-knit towns, and quiet pride characterize many Mid-Atlantic mining towns. A West Virginia town's mural expresses these traits.

RICHWOOD MONUMENTS 8462000

What kind of work?

Workers in the Mid-Atlantic include many dockworkers, steelworkers, mechanics, and carpenters. They are called "blue collar workers." Teachers, salespeople, and secretaries are examples of "white collar workers." Service workers include nurses, cashiers, and police who assist people directly. In the Mid-Atlantic, service and white collar jobs are increasing fastest.

Factories and owners

A **corporation** is a form of company that allows several owners. It is highly organized with many levels of managers. The key to corporations' success is the huge amounts of money that can be raised. United States Steel, The New York Times, and Norfolk Southern Railroad are examples of Mid-Atlantic corporations with thousands of owners. Some of the region's other large corporations involve electronics, chemicals, processed foods, financial services, oil refining, publishing, advertising, and entertainment.

The steel industry is an important industry in the Mid-Atlantic region.

Chemical companies

Like the electrical industry, chemical production employs hundreds of thousands of workers in the Mid-Atlantic. Large chemical companies in the region produce a wide variety of goods including plastics, camera film, cement, paint, and textiles. Because these products require many parts and ingredients, most companies are located near harbors where raw materials can be easily brought into the region.

DuPont, headquartered in Wilmington, Delaware, is the largest chemical company in the world. To remain competitive, chemical companies have to constantly study ways to produce new and better products.

DuPont laboratories are an example of the trend toward technology and chemical industries in the region.
▼

Publishing center

The Mid-Atlantic states produce more books than any other region of the United States. This is a particularly big business in New York City. Check the first few pages of books in your library and you will see that many were published in a city of this region.

Free Time

On Broadway

Broadway is the street that lies at the heart of New York City's theater district. Plays and musicals on Broadway are among the most popular for tourists. Some may run for years. Shows that are off-Broadway may be popular, too. But seeing a show on Broadway is often the highlight of a visit to New York City.

The Mid-Atlantic is home to many great artists, actors, and musicians. Several acting schools, art schools, and opportunities to perform in theaters are found in the region.

There are so many famous actors and musicians from or living in the Mid-Atlantic that it is difficult to list them all. For example, the following people were born in New York City alone: Christina Aguilera, Robert de Niro, P. Diddy, Vin Diesel, 50 Cent, Cuba Gooding Jr., Jay-Z, Norah Jones, Lindsay Lohan, Jennifer Lopez, Eddie Murphy, Jack Nicholson, Adam Sandler, and Jerry Seinfeld.

Times Square in New York City is alive at all hours of the day. Entertainment and shopping are major activities.

The Smithsonian

Large cities of the Mid-Atlantic are known for having great museums. The Smithsonian Institution in Washington DC operates eighteen museums including the National Museum of Natural History, the Air and Space Museum, and the National Museum of American History. At these sites, visitors can see exhibits such as one of the world's most valuable diamonds, sets from famous TV shows, and bones of prehistoric creatures.

Artistic areas

Much artistic expression occurs outside of the Mid-Atlantic's huge cities. Rochester, New York, and its surrounding areas are known for having great artistic communities and excellent places to study art. Traditional arts and crafts also flourish in Appalachian areas of West Virginia, Maryland, and Virginia.

Metropolitan Museum of Art

The New York Metropolitan Museum of Art has something for everyone. Besides paintings, visitors can see beautiful clothing, portraits of presidents, great photos, Chinese jewelry, and tools from Africa. For students, there are sketching classes and storytelling. There are even valuable musical instruments and stained-glass windows on display.

The Andy Warhol Museum in Pittsburgh, Pennsylvania, houses many of the famous artist's works.

Spreading apples

Mid-Atlantic states grow great amounts of apples. Apple butter on bread is a favorite among rural people in the region. Apple butter is often made and sold as a fundraiser by organizations. Peeled, sliced, and cleaned, apples are slowly cooked in large containers. Large paddles constantly stir the pasty apple butter that forms. Sweet, healthy, and delicious, it rarely lasts long in Mid-Atlantic households.

Food

The Mid-Atlantic's international population makes it easy to find a variety of food choices. The region offers everything from legendary sandwiches to gourmet dishes.

Maryland crab

One delicious choice from the area is crab dishes. Fresh from bays like the Chesapeake, people in Maryland and nearby states enjoy this food on a regular basis. Formed into small patties called crab cakes, it is a huge favorite grilled, fried, or mixed with other foods.

Delicious dishes featuring crabmeat are displayed during a cooking competition.
▼

Cultural mix

New York City is famous for its fine-dining restaurants and great delicatessens, or delis. Some of the greatest chefs in the world can be found in its restaurants. Because so many different ethnic groups live in New York, many types of ethnic foods are available there. For example, Polish, Italian, and Jewish delicatessens each serve different types of sandwiches and sell different types of food.

"Philly" cheese steak sandwiches are another regional favorite. Long sandwich buns are loaded with steak, melted cheese, and several toppings to make Philadelphia's most famous food. Delicatessens have annual competitions to see who can make the best-tasting cheese steak.

Hershey's home

Milton Hershey established Hershey Chocolate Company in 1905. It was an immediate success and became the first chocolate to be sold all over the United States. Four years later, Hershey established a school for orphan boys and soon donated almost all of his profits from the company to the school. More than 1,000 boys and girls now attend this school in Hershey, Pennsylvania.

For almost 400 years, Virginians have produced hams. Smoking and seasoning the meat properly has become an art in itself.

43

Team passion

Baseball, football, basketball, ice hockey, and golf are the most popular sports of the Mid-Atlantic. Spectators fill arenas to see the New York Yankees play baseball, Philadelphia 76ers play basketball, New Jersey Devils play hockey, or the Pittsburgh Steelers play football. Fans in the region follow their favorite teams with passion. They also enjoy watching and playing golf.

Lacrosse

One sport played at the high school and college levels much more in the Mid-Atlantic than other regions is lacrosse (above). This game was first played by Native Americans. Players attempt to get a ball into a goal using a long stick with netting. The national college champion in lacrosse often comes from a Mid-Atlantic university.

The New York Knicks play their home basketball games in Madison Square Garden in New York City.
▼

Playing sports

Not everyone can play for the Pittsburgh Steelers, but almost everyone can participate in some sport. Almost every town has a number of city parks and golf courses that people can enjoy. Likewise, people enjoy hiking on trails in West Virginia's George Washington National Forest, along the scenic Hudson River in New York, or on the amber-colored beaches of Delaware.

Residents living in Washington DC can drive about one hour and enjoy a hike on mountain trails. This is part of the attraction for people to live in the Mid-Atlantic—it has the best of both city and country lifestyles. In winter many people in the Mid-Atlantic ski at resorts or skate on ice rinks found throughout the region.

Hiking is a popular outdoor sport in places such as Shenandoah National Park in Virginia.
▾

Rock climbing

At Seneca Rocks, West Virginia, rock climbers scale 900-foot (275-meter) cliffs. The cliffs jut almost straight up toward the sky. Like solving a puzzle, climbers scale rock walls going from hand-hold to hand-hold. Finding a good route is important. When climbers reach the top, they are rewarded with a beautiful view and a feeling of accomplishment.

Underground music

Portions of the Mid-Atlantic have large caverns. One of the most famous is Luray Caverns, located in the Shenandoah Valley of Virginia. Colorful orange, yellow, and white rock formations can be seen, along with an underground organ. It uses an intricate system of small hammers to strike various rocks that make musical sounds. It really works. It even supplies music for weddings held inside the cavern!

Keeping it cool

For many Mid-Atlantic residents, nothing compares to sailing. On most weekends, sailboats can be seen everywhere on the Chesapeake Bay and other area waters. Sailboat masts crowd **marinas** in places such as Annapolis, Maryland. People in the region also enjoy splashing through rapids on the Potomac River or rushing streams. The area has a wide variety of recreational sites available, including Virginia's Shenandoah National Park, Delaware's Rehoboth Beach, and West Virginia's Snowshoe Ski Resort.

For those with a sense of adventure, whitewater rafting awaits. Several rivers plunge down slopes in the Mid-Atlantic. A remote but popular rafting site is the Smoke Hole in West Virginia.

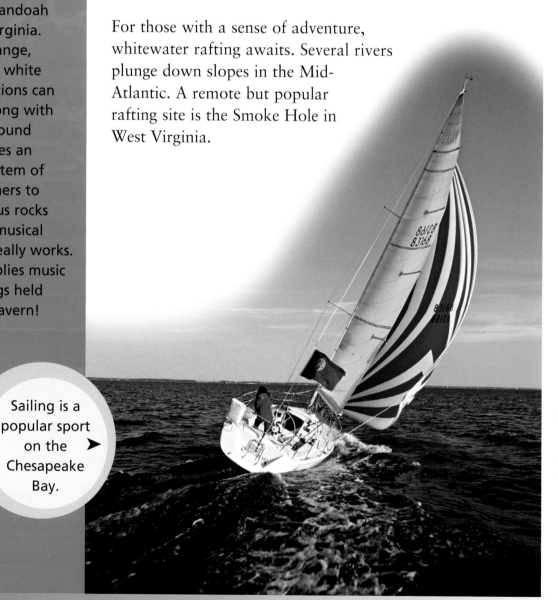

Sailing is a popular sport on the ➤ Chesapeake Bay.

Favorite outdoor sites

A beautiful portion of the Appalachian Trail passes through New York, Pennsylvania, Maryland, and Virginia. Each year, millions of Mid-Atlantic residents hike parts of the trail, such as the part passing through Harper's Ferry, West Virginia. Here the Shenandoah River rushes into the Potomac between majestic, steep-sloped mountains.

True amusement

The Mid-Atlantic states have many amusement parks. The first important one in the country was Coney Island in the New York City area. It is still in operation today. Because of the large regional population and moderate climate, several other outdoor amusement parks have located to the area.

Coney Island is the oldest amusement park on the East Coast. It is still popular today.

Thrilling rides

What are the most popular rides of the many Mid-Atlantic amusement parks? Astroland's "Cyclone" wooden roller coaster at Coney Island, New York; "Superman: Ride of Steel" roller coaster at Six Flags Darien Lake, New York; and Kennywood's "Phantom's Revenge" roller coaster in Pittsburgh are some of the top choices. The Mid-Atlantic region has more than 40 theme and amusement parks.

Festivals of art

Large and small cities in the Mid-Atlantic show the works of local artists at special festivals. These are especially popular during warm months when art can be shown outdoors. Cities and towns have such events in town squares, parks, or on waterfronts.

Festivals and holidays

Mid-Atlantic residents love to celebrate. The most popular holidays are historic ones, New Year's Day, and days that celebrate people's heritage. Independence Day, which celebrates the beginning of the United States, is also popular. It's no surprise that Philadelphia, where the Declaration of Independence was written and adopted, is the site of huge celebrations every Fourth of July. Reenactments, fireworks displays, parades, and many special events are held.

Hundreds of thousands of people crowd New York City's Times Square each New Year's Eve. They watch a huge lighted ball drop and announce the New Year. Televised nationwide, New York is the focus for this holiday ritual.

The New Year's Day Parade in Philadelphia features colorful and creative costumes.

48

Holidays that remember

Many events in the Mid-Atlantic region are held in memory of the sacrifices women and men of the United States military made. Stirring ceremonies regularly occur at Arlington Cemetery near Washington DC. This is where many soldiers who have died for the country are buried.

Because there are immigrants from so many different countries living in the Mid-Atlantic, ethnic holidays are also celebrated throughout the region. In this way, ethnic groups celebrate their heritage as well as sharing it with other people in the region.

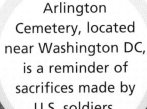

Arlington Cemetery, located near Washington DC, is a reminder of sacrifices made by U.S. soldiers.
▼

In memory of

More than 300,000 men lost their lives in Virginia during the Civil War. Richmond, Virginia, was the Confederacy's capital city and Union forces constantly marched into the state. Numerous reenactments are held at battlefield sites in the state. "Re-enactors" in authentic uniforms attempt to replicate the huge battles fought there.

An Amazing Region

Chesapeake Bay

The Chesapeake Bay is one of the largest bays located in the United States. It is also one of the nation's most useful water areas. Used for fishing, recreation, and as a great location for harbor cities, it runs north to south between portions of Virginia and Maryland.

The Mid-Atlantic states play an important role for the United States. They possess more harbor locations, business headquarters, and large cities than any other region. In part this is because the area has many transportation advantages.

Bays and rivers provide ports in the area. A lack of mountains near the East Coast makes land transportation in the region easier. The Mid-Atlantic is also rich in natural resources. When these factors are combined, it is easy to see why many companies want to locate in the Mid-Atlantic.

The Mid-Atlantic began and continues today as a beautiful area for farming. Natural beauty and human industry truly blend in this region.

▼

Meeting challenges

Some states in the Mid-Atlantic such as New York, New Jersey, and Pennsylvania are meeting new challenges. For example, some states are facing problems associated with overcrowding, pollution, traffic, and crime. Despite the overcrowding, people living in the megalopolis have many advantages.

Nowhere else in the United States can people find the amounts of jobs, cultural attractions, entertainment options, and beautiful scenery as in the Mid-Atlantic. It is the people of the region who make it successful. The Mid-Atlantic's future depends on its **multicultural** population supplying new ideas, better methods, and hard work.

Mid-Atlantic cities have always been important to the United States. Pittsburgh and other urban areas of the region also strive to improve living conditions.

A city for living

An example of the ability of Mid-Atlantic people to adapt and succeed can be found in Charlottesville, Virginia. Best known as Thomas Jefferson's birthplace and site for the University of Virginia, it faced many tough challenges through the years. Shallow rivers, lack of raw materials, and the effects of the Civil War all limited industrial development. But hard work by citizens resulted in a beautiful city that was creative in attracting businesses. In 2005 a major travel publication named it the "best place to live in America."

Find Out More

World Wide Web

The Fifty States
www.infoplease. com/states.html
This website has a clickable U.S. map that gives facts about each of the 50 states, plus images of each state's flag. These sites have pictures, statistics, and other facts about each state in the Mid-Atlantic region:
Are We There Yet? New Jersey
www.fieldtrip.com/nj
Fun for Kids in Virginia
www.funforkids. virginia.cc
Maryland Kids page
www.MDkidspage.org
New York State for Kids
http://www.iloveny. com/kids/index.asp
Pennsylvania Visitor's Network
http://pavisitnet.com/ kids/
State of Delaware Kids' Page
http://www.state.de.us. /gic/kidspage/
West Virginia Wild and Wonderful
http://www.wvtourism. com/

Books to read

Bjorlund, Lydia. *Indigenous Peoples of North America: The Iroquois.* San Diego: Lucent Books, 2001.

Blashfield, Jean F. *America the Beautiful: Delaware.* New York: Children's Press, Grolier Publishing, 2000.

Heinrichs, Ann. *Maryland.* Minneapolis: Compass Point Books, 2003.

Moragne, Wendy. *Celebrate the States: New Jersey.* New York: Benchmark Books, Marshall Cavendish, 2000.

Smith, Karla. *Unique Virginia.* Chicago: Heinemann Library, 2003.

Swain, Gwenyth. *Pennsylvania: Hello U.S.A.* Minneapolis: Lerner Publications, 2002.

Historic places to visit

Colonial Williamsburg (Williamsburg, Virginia) This is an authentic Colonial capital city.

Delaware History Museum (Wilmington, Delaware) Explores the history of Delaware.

Ellis Island (New York, New York) Site for immigrant arrivals and evaluation.

Fort McHenry (Baltimore, Maryland) Site of the 1814 battle that was the subject for the U.S. national anthem.

Gettysburg National Battlefield (Gettysburg, Pennsylvania) Explore the location of the largest battle of the Civil War.

Grave Creek Mound Archaeology Complex (Moundsville, West Virginia) This is the site of Native American burial mounds.

Menlo Park Museum (Edison, New Jersey) Explores Thomas Edison's laboratory.

Timeline

1570
Iroquois form League of Five Nations.

1607
English found Jamestown in what is now Virginia.

1619
First democratically-elected legislature in North America meets in Jamestown, Virginia.

1756–1763
French and Indian War brings fighting to New York, Pennsylvania, and Virginia.

1775
Quakers establish the first anti-slavery group in the United States.

1775–1783
Revolutionary War—many major battles fought in Mid-Atlantic areas.

1776
Declaration of Independence adopted in Philadelphia.

1818
The National Road, the first federally-funded highway, is finished from Baltimore to Wheeling, Virginia (now in West Virginia).

1813
Francis Scott Key writes the "Star-Spangled Banner" while aboard a ship during the bombardment of Baltimore by the British.

1800
Washington DC becomes the new capital city of the United States.

1789–1800
United States capital is established first at New York and then in Philadelphia.

1787
US Constitution is written in Philadelphia.

1777
Large British army surrenders to Colonials at Saratoga, New York.

1825
Erie Canal is finished across New York State linking the Hudson River with Lake Ontario.

1861–1865
Civil War is fought. Hundreds of thousands die on battlefields in the region.

1863
West Virginia secedes from Virginia. Battle of Gettysburg is fought in Pennsylvania.

1865
President Lincoln assassinated at Ford's Theatre, Washington DC.

1876
Centennial Exposition held in Philadelphia.

1879
Thomas Edison invents the incandescent light bulb in New Jersey.

1883
New York's Brooklyn Bridge is completed.

2001
Terrorists crash planes into New York City's World Trade Towers and Washington DC's Pentagon building. Fourth plane crashes in southern Pennsylvania.

1979
Three Mile Island nuclear power plant accident occurs in Pennsylvania.

1947
Brooklyn Dodgers' Jackie Robinson becomes the first African American to play Major League Baseball.

1932
Franklin D. Roosevelt of New York is elected president, and serves longer than any other U.S. president in history.

1931
Empire State Building is completed in New York City.

1929
New York Stock Market "crashes," setting off the Great Depression.

States at a Glance

Delaware
Nickname: Diamond State
Became State: 1787
Capital: Dover
Motto: Liberty and Independence
Bird: Blue hen chicken
Tree: American holly
Flower: Peach blossom
Animal: None
Song: "Our Delaware"

Maryland
Nickname: Old Line State
Became State: 1788
Capital: Annapolis
Motto: Manly deeds, womanly words
Bird: Baltimore oriole
Tree: White oak
Flower: Black-eyed Susan
Animal: None
Song: "Maryland, my Maryland"

New Jersey
Nickname: Garden State
Became State: 1787
Capital: Trenton
Motto: Liberty and Prosperity
Bird: Eastern goldfinch
Tree: Red oak
Flower: Violet
Animal: Horse
Song: "I'm from New Jersey"

New York
Nickname: Empire State
Became State: 1788
Capital: Albany
Motto: Ever Upward
Bird: Bluebird
Tree: Sugar maple
Flower: Rose
Animal: Beaver
Song: "I Love New York"

Pennsylvania
Nickname: Keystone State
Became State: 1787
Capital: Harrisburg
Motto: Virtue, Liberty, and Independence
Bird: Ruffed grouse
Tree: Eastern hemlock
Flower: Mountain laurel
Animal: Whitetail deer
Song: "Pennsylvania"

Virginia
Nickname: The Old Dominion
Became State: 1788
Capital: Richmond
Motto: Thus always to tyrants
Bird: Cardinal
Tree: Dogwood tree
Flower: Dogwood bloom
Animal: None
Song: "Carry Me Back to Old Virginia"

West Virginia
Nickname: The Mountain State
Became State: 1863
Capital: Charleston
Motto: Mountaineers are always free
Bird: Cardinal
Tree: Sugar maple
Flower: Rhododendron
Animal: Black bear
Song: "The West Virginia Hills"

Glossary

Amish religious group whose followers settled in Pennsylvania in the 1700s

border dividing line between one country or region and another

borough one of five areas New York City is divided into

canopy roof-like shelter formed by the leaves of trees

cluster group of similar things

commute travel back and forth, usually to work

Confederate part of the government formed by states in the South during the Civil War

corporation large company in which shareholders (owners) divide expenses and profits

descendants people who come from those before them

estuary (more than one are called estuaries) wide area at the ends of rivers

ethnic group collection of people that have similar cultural backgrounds

flash flood sudden flooding after a heavy rain

foreign policy relations with other countries

French and Indian War war fought in North America between England and France involving Native Americans allied with France (1754–1763)

green space park-lands and other natural settings

habitat correct place for a person or animal to live

immigrants people who come into a nation to live

Industrial Revolution time when new machines began to replace human and animal power

invasive species plants and animals from other lands

lake-effect snow heavy snow caused by a cold area picking up large amounts of moisture from large lakes

marina place where pleasure boats can be secured in a harbor

megalopolis huge chain of cities that have grown together

mouth where a river empties into another body of water

multicultural of many cultures

natural resource useful material from nature

New York Stock Exchange site where shares of companies are bought and sold

plateau high, flat area of land

precipitation moisture falling to earth as rain, snow, sleet, freezing rain, or hail

produce fresh fruits and vegetables

Quaker religious group whose members try to live simply

radioactive gas poisonous vapor

raw material unfinished product used to make a usable good

renewable capable of being replaced

seaport harbor where ships are loaded or unloaded

suburb residential area near, but not inside a city

tanning process of making leather from animal hides

Union name for the United States during the Civil War

United Nations international organization of countries set up to work toward international security, peace, and cooperation

urban crowded, city area

wetland coastal marsh that is swampy and has tall grasses

Index